THE SOUTHERN HIGHLANDS
OF SCOTLAND

Red Kite

Photography by
GRAEME WALLACE

First published in Great Britain 2013

Designed & Artwork by Kevin Jeffery

Printed in China

Published by

GW Publishing
PO Box 15070,
Dunblane,
FK15 5AN

www.gwpublishing.com

ISBN 978-0-9570844-4-5

Photograph on page 4 taken by Dave Kirkpatrick, who has patiently joined me and been a great companion on numerous trips.

Map on page 12 supplied by Global Mapping (www.globalmapping.uk.com) Data ©The XYX Digital Map Company

**To order prints of images in this book visit
www.graemewallaceprints.com**

CONTENTS

The photographs in this book are presented in the order of the month in which they were taken over a period of five years. Showing the unpredictability of the weather and how much it can vary out of season, the images in this book show that the seasons don't always comply with the months in which they are expected. This is particularly so for winter which can sometimes arrive with a vengeance in November and can linger on the hill tops through to April. 2012 was no exception to the unpredictability of the weather. After a good snowfall in early December 2011, there was very little precipitation through January and February, followed by a heat wave in March and numerous further heavy snowfalls in April.

MOUNTAIN PHOTOGRAPHY

Whenever I take a landscape photograph, creativity is very much at the forefront of my mind. While there is always an element of luck in getting a great photo, simply by being in the right place at the right time, I always stop and take time to think about how the view can be improved: 'what can I do to make it different?' Can I achieve a better-balance image or accentuate the depth and drama by moving my position a few paces or crouching lower to the ground, or by including an extra element into the picture, for example? Always striving to create rather than just capture.

Planning and preparation are vital to successful photography in the mountain and anticipating the weather and lighting conditions is key. I generally set out with a specific idea in mind, both in terms of the view I intend to photograph and the conditions I am seeking. It may be a sunrise, a cloud inversion, a heavy storm, long shadows or a feeling of isolation, but each photograph is pre-created in my mind. That said, there are plenty of times when the envisaged photograph does not go according to plan and I end up with a completely different scene. Consequently, being constantly aware of the surrounding landscape is vital to a successful outing.

All the main photographs in this book were taken on a Hasselblad Xpan using Fuji Provia 100 film.

With the best preparation in the world, no-one can know exactly what the weather will do. This is particularly the case for mountain regions which often create their own unique weather conditions. For me, the most interesting photographs are those with a good deal of cloud and a little sunlight. Needless to say, getting the sun to highlight a specific summit or lochan while dark clouds brood overhead, casting patches of shadow across the landscape, requires immense patience and considerable perseverance.

The Scottish Highland weather is one of the most challenging of all mountain regions, notorious for its unpredictability and unsettledness. Experiencing numerous seasons in one day is not uncommon, even in late spring, while the summer months bring few guarantees of settled conditions. It is this changeability that is the essential ingredient for creating unique photographs however, impossible to replicate, and is the essence of stirring and provocative landscapes.

Creating the images I have in mind usually requires early morning starts or late evening finishes, often travelling up or down a mountain with a head torch lighting the way for a couple of hours of the journey. Alternatively, sleeping on the summits guarantees I'm in the right place at the right time, although even then there is still no guarantee of the outcome
. Travelling with a good weathproof tent and supplies in addition to camera gear does make for a demanding slog and is not embarked on without some assurance of the desired weather.

Prior to an overnight camp or torch-lit trek, I usually visit a location in good daylight conditions first in order to determine where best to photograph, learn the trail and make myself aware of any hazards. Its rare to find me up a mountain during heavy rain and low cloud as the conditions are totally unsuitable for photography and I don't particularly enjoy getting wet! However, as stated earlier, the Scottish mountain weather is unpredictable and I'm generally out when there is some risk of poor weather. So having the correct clothing and navigational experience is vital, particularly as I usually travel alone.

While rain, snow and cold present clear and obvious hazards, it is low cloud that can be the greatest danger. Cloud can unexpectedly appear over the tops of mountain at any time of year, creating poor (sometimes zero) visibility. Low cloud also means some precipitation, further hampering visibility, and adding to a sense of urgency which in turn can lead to panic and injury. Even a popular and 'friendly' Munro like Ben Lomond has a steep and dangerous rocky face on its northeast side which could prove deadly if a walker were to become disorientated. Preparation, care and respect are vital to enjoining them at their most evocative and telling. If approached correctly, they offer truly lifetime experiences.

INTRODUCTION

The Southern Highlands of Scotland incorporate the region of land stretching from Loch Lomond in the southwest up to Loch Tummel in Perthshire, central Scotland. In fact, a direct line can be drawn from north of Glasgow, through Perthshire and across to Stonehaven on the east coast, following the Highland Boundary Line demarking the Highlands from the Lowlands. The land immediately to the north of this Highland Boundary Line along as far as Perth is the Southern Highlands. A roughly parallel line from Dalmally to Pitlochry marks its northern perimeter with the Central Highland region.

Although not as imposing as some of the more northerly landscapes, the Southern Highlands are still rugged and wild, dramatic and enchanting. Despite its close proximity to Scotland's large population belt, an hour's drive can lead to solitude and tranquillity. For many visitors, the Southern Highlands are their first and only experience of Scotland's mountain region and it does a fine job of depicting the vast Highland region. There are many lochs and glens to discover either by road, track and boat or, for the more intrepid, on foot. Trudging across the bouldery and often boggy land is the best way of accessing the remotest locations and highest summits.

It may come as a surprise to learn that there are 46 Munros (Scottish mountains over 915 m or 3000 ft) scattered across the loch-strewn area of the Southern Highlands. Central to the area is Ben Lawers which, at 1214 m, is the tenth-highest Munro in Scotland.

The most famous mountain in the Southern Highlands (if not the whole of Scotland) is Ben Lomond, standing at 974 m along the eastern shoreline of Loch Lomond. Unmistakable from the western main road it is the most southerly Munro and a very popular destination for hill walkers, particularly for nearby Glaswegians who have adopted it as their hill. Similarly, Schiehallion at 1083 m is the most north-easterly Munro in the area and is a very popular climb with locals from nearby Perth. Both mountains are solitary, standing alone beyond the ranges and can thus be identified from the summit of Munros many miles away.

Much of the area is managed by Loch Lomond and The Trossachs National Park. Although only

Loch Lomond

established in 2002 it encompasses numerous older park areas, including the Argyll Forest established over 75 years ago and the Queen Elizabeth Forest established over 50 years ago. The enlarged park is 1865 km2 (720 square miles) and incorporates approximately half the Munros and the majority of the larger lochs.

Although the area is managed by Loch Lomond and The Trossachs National Park, Ben Lomond together with numerous other Munros are owned by the National Trust for Scotland. Also owned by the National Trust for Scotland is the Ben Lawers Range which falls outside the National Park, but is protected within the Ben Lawers National Nature Reserve primarily due to the rare flora that survives on the mountainsides.

BEN LOMOND AND THE ARROCHAR ALPS

Ben Lomond's fame is no doubt due to its location midway up Loch Lomond, on the opposite side to the main road north from Glasgow to Fort William and Inverness. Its unmistakable profile as seen from the south and west, and its position of relative solitude give it an air of grandeur and dignity. Its long broad southerly sloping ridge makes it a relatively easy climb, while its north face is sharp and chiselled giving it a more dramatic alpine appearance. Although a "tamed" hill, as with all other Munros it deserves respect, particularly in inclement weather which can arrive unannounced at any time of year.

Meall nan Tarmachan

On the opposite side of Loch Lomond are the Arrochar Alps. This compact group of four Munros are, for the most part, hidden behind the foothills which bear down on the twisting loch-shore road. They are best viewed from the car park at Inveruglas or across the loch from Inversnaid. An alterative view can be enjoyed from the village of Arrochar and alongside Loch Long, west of Tarbet. The most prominent feature from here is the craggy ridge line of Ben Arthur, better known as The Cobbler. While The Cobbler is 30 m shy of qualifying as a Munro, it is still a very popular destination for climbers with the challenge of its exposed and precariously upright pinnacle providing a final test of nerve and skill.

The most westerly Munro in the Southern Highlands is Beinn Bhuidhe. Hidden quite some way up Glen Fyne (but clearly visible from the west), it provides great views south along Loch Fyne and the Kintyre peninsula.

Loch Lomond is land-locked and, at over 24 miles long, enjoys the acclaim of being the largest loch in Scotland by surface area. With approximately 60 islands on the loch, it also boasts the largest freshwater island in the British Isles. Running across the southern end of the loch, the Highland Boundary Line adjoins the islands of Inchmurrin, Creinch, Torrinch and Inchcailloch across to Balmaha and beyond to Stonehaven on the east coast. Everything north of the line is considered the Highland of Scotland.

While some islands such as Inchmurrin (the largest) once had whole communities living on them and are still frequently visited, others further up the loch hardly receive a second glance and remain largely undisturbed. Some of these very small islands have however provided a safe retreat for clan-folk in the past and, upon closer inspection, reveal the ruins of castles that once stood proud (and in some cases occupied the bulk of the island).

The loch is 5 miles across at its widest part in the south and becomes increasingly narrower as it cuts into an ever-deepening glen, offering superb views from all sides. Some of the finest views are from vantage points at the north end of the loch, from where it can be seen snaking down the numerous rocky outcrops and narrowing around tiny islands before flowing to Ben Lomond and beyond.

THE TROSSACHS

The Trossachs are known as Rob Roy Macgregor country and have been made famous by Sir Walter Scott's storybooks based around the area. The largest loch is Loch Katrine which is the primary source of water for Glasgow, Scotland's largest city 20 miles away. The south end of the loch is the hub of activity for people wishing to see the area by steamer, bicycle or on foot. Similar to Loch Lomond, the larger islands are to the south of the loch and somewhat obscure the tranquil glen beyond. A boat cruise or trip along the north-eastern shore makes a very pleasant half-day excursion and leads to the very heart of Macgregor territory.

Loch Venachar

Despite William Wordsworth's wife Dorothy reputedly claiming that the north end of the loch was not as romantically beautiful as the south, it is for me the more appealing. With a rugged and remote charm, it is here where Rob Roy was born. Although remote, it was a major thoroughfare with a vital drover's road bringing cattle over from the head of Loch Lomond, down through Glen Gyle and along Loch Katrine south to market.

An alternative route to the head of Loch Katrine is via the picturesque village of Aberfoyle and the meandering road past several other smaller, but beautifully situated, lochs that make up much of the Trossachs.

THE CRIANLARICH HILLS

North of Loch Katrine and Loch Lomond are the Crianlarich Hills. A group of seven adjoining Munros, the most northerly and the highest is Ben More at 1174 m. Immediately behind Ben More is its flat-topped partner Stob Binnein; the pair provide a useful bearing from the surrounding summits and, indeed, from the roads leading to Crianlarich from the east and the north. The remaining Munros lie to the southwest of the village, presenting an evocative backdrop to the sparse clusters of Caledonian pine along brooding Glen Falloch. Each of these Munros have character and grandeur and hide behind long and craggy north-westerly facing ridges. Names such as An Caisteal and Twistin Hill say it all.

Ben Lawers

THE TYNDRUM HILLS

To the west of Crianlarich are the four Munros of Tyndrum, the highest and most prominent of which is Ben Laoigh ('Lui') at 1130 m. Extremely popular with climbers, its steep northeast-facing coire presents a satisfying scramble with the iced-up Centra Gully becoming a magnet for ice climbers looking to make a more direct assent to the summit in winter. Facing northeast, the vertical gully holds onto any snow well into the spring and its prominent chiselled features make it one of the most dramatic mountain faces in Scotland.

A little to the east of Ben Lui and directly north of Loch Lomond is Beinn Dubhchraig. It provides a fantastic view down the glen, particularly in high summer when the setting sun creates strong highlights and shadows, emphasising the hills and ridges breaking the endless shoreline of the loch.

THE BRIDGE OF ORCHY HILLS

North of Crianlarich and Tyndrum is Bridge of Orchy. The Munros here once marked the boundary between the Dalriadic Kingdom of the Scots and their eastern Pictish neighbours and the Kingdom of Alba. Now they simply form the northern boundary of the Southern Highlands. The five Munros are all to the east of the road, with Beinn Dorain dominating the view from the tiny settlement. In March 2011, I decided to head up Beinn Dorain in the expectation that the weather would turn for the better and present a snow-covered landscape around Loch Tulla. It did not. It turned for the worse in fact with the cloud lowering to about 600 m, resulting in a dreadfully driech afternoon. The constant drizzle was compounded by heavily thawing snow and extremely boggy ground underfoot. The result was a total soaking and an extremely frustrating day. A bad call but, when striving for atmospheric views, a clear blue cloudless sky would have been equally disappointing.

I made a better call for the same location later in the year when setting off to Loch Tulla, which lies just beyond Bridge of Orchy. Loch Tulla is a particularly photogenic loch with a scattering of islands, twisted Caledonian pine trees and Munros in three directions. I was determined to get the perfect shot from here across to the Bridge of Orchy Hills in the east, so arrived on a glorious autumn day and in good time before the sun went down behind me. The weather did cooperate this time, resulting in one of my most pleasing shots.

The road from Bridge of Orchy continues on north to Glencoe and the Central Highlands, which is another book. It is however worth noting that as the road snakes on up towards Rannoch Moor there is a lay-by at the top of the hill providing a great vantage point with views to the south over Loch Tulla, to the Bridge of Orchy Munros and beyond to many of the Southern Highlands.

Ben Glas waterfall

THE MAMLORN HILLS

The Munros immediately to the east of Crianlarich are the Mamlorns, standing guard over what was once a great hunting forest. The Mamlorn Hills lie hidden at the head of Glen Lochay, a quiet and pretty glen in which the River Lochay twists, turns and tumbles through wooded copse all the way back to the village of Killin where it joins the River Dochart at the mouth of Loch Tay.

In the shadow of the Tarmachan Ridge, the Falls of Dochart at Killin are one of the most impressive falls in Scotland. Rugged and powerful, they are particularly stunning in the autumn months when the foliage is in full colour. Prior to reaching the peaceful waters of Loch Tay, the River Dochart battles over a series of rapids while navigating its way around either side of a tree-clad island, past an old waterwheel, through a narrowing gorge, under a dual arched stone bridge and then splits again around a second large island, the ancient burial ground of Clan MacNab.

THE LAWERS GROUP

A glimpse of some of the eight peaks that make up the Lawers Group can be had from Killin. Clearest in view is the undulating and popular western ridge of Meal nan Tarmachan at 1044 m. Beyond it are the five Munros that make up the long ridge of Ben Lawers which dominate much of the northern shore line of Loch Tay. Ben Lawers at 1214 m is huge and tops the others summits, although An Stuc at 1118 m is the most dramatic when viewed from a higher elevation.

The heavy snowfall at the end of 2009 presented major traffic problems for Scottish commuters, but the perfect opportunity to capture the long Lawers ridge over Loch Tay. Clear air and fresh snow highlighted the peaks and emphasised the drama of the landscape. Getting to a good viewpoint in deep snow along the road on the southern side of the loch was touch and go at times, but proved worthwhile with a magnificent landscape showing the mountain range at its finest.

With good access, I have climbed the Lawers hills more than any other in the Southern Highlands; on every occasion the weather has proven changeable and unpredictable. Despite considerable preparation and the best planning there is always the chance that the weather will not cooperate; it is this ever-changing weather that results in the most captivating photographs and is an inherent part of landscape photography. Disillusionment and frustration are common, but the reward and satisfaction when a shot does go as planned more than make up for the disappointments.

One such case was a trek up icy Beinn Ghlas towards the end of a cold mid-winter's day. Despite driving winds gusting at up to 100 mph, the cloud sitting over Beinn Ghlas and Ben Lawers appeared as if it was there to stay. However, with the knowledge that the clouds often disperse towards the end of the day and in the belief that this would happen, I set off positive and hopeful. Within minutes of reaching the summit, the cloud did indeed clear just long enough to get a great shot. While I did not get the sunset I had planned on, I did capture my most memorable photograph in the book looking north along the glen and the Allt a' Chobhair burn. This more than made up for numerous other 'failed' trips up this Munro.

Highland Cow on Conic Hil

In addition to its acclaim of being a high mountain ridge, the Lawers hills also incorporate a National Nature Reserve. The lime-rich soil on its slopes means that delicate arctic and alpine plants such as Alpine Saxifrage, Mouse-ear and Fleabane thrive here through the spring and summer months. A well marked trail aids the viewing these wild flowers.

LOCH EARN HILLS

To the south of Loch Tay are a number of smaller lochs, each one picturesque and unique. Loch Earn is the largest and is overlooked by two Munros while Loch Voil and Loch Doine lead into the heart of the Crianlarich Hills along the River Larig. Rob Roy Macgregor is buried in the picturesque churchyard at Balquhidder to the east of Loch Voil, beyond which the glen leads into remote Macgregor country.

Having a reputation as being one of the easier Munros, Ben Vorlich above Loch Earn was the first winter climb I undertook. Kitted out with full winter gear including crampons and ice axe together with a full pack of camera equipment, the assent was fairly steady although still demanding. I felt somewhat over-equipped, however, as I watched children glide past on sledges and make-shift snowboards. Nevertheless, the ice equipment was needed with the final 300 m being considerably steeper and icier. On this first trip I did not get a worthy photograph, but it was a useful reconnaissance exercise and set the way for a number of other assents (including a successful overnight camp on the summit in midsummer and a very pleasing sunrise over Loch Earn).

GLEN LYON AND RANNOCH HILLS

Considered by some as the most beautiful glen in Scotland, Glen Lyon is long and leads to the two remote lochs of Loch Lyon and Loch an Daimh. The later is the higher and feels more isolated with steep walls on three sides. Loch an Daimh has a Munro standing either side of it, both of which offer great views, however it is the hills at the south end of the loch that provide the finest view back along the glen.

The four Munros of Glen Lyon are actually reached way before the loch and are not best positioned for loch views. However, the glen travels deep inland and is overlooked by the Munros of the Mamlorns and Bridge of Orchy in the west. My favourite viewpoint is from Beinn a' Chaistell at the head of the loch which, although a little shy of Munro stature, is high enough to provide stunning mountain-top views in all directions.

To the east of Glen Lyon lies the quaint hamlet of Fortingall. More Hampshire than Highlands, the thatched cottages are part of a 'planned' village built close by the historic church. Fortingall is best know for its ancient Yew tree, believed to be 2000–5000 years old and planted during the Iron Age on a sacred site.

Last but certainly not least is Schiehallion at 1083 m. Like Ben Lomond, it stands alone. The most north-easterly of the Southern Highlands, Schiehallion has an easily distinguishable pyramid shape and can be picked out from Munro tops a great distance away and from the roads leading to it from all directions.

Loch Tummel, Loch Rannoch and the remote Rannoch Train Station mark the northerly boundary for the Munros of the Southern Highlands, while the northwest is demarked by the open expanse of Rannoch Moor leading to the Central Highlands of Ben Nevis and Glen Coe. Made famous by Queen Victoria, Queen's View at the eastern end of Loch Tummel provides an ideal point from which to view Schiehallion and the end of the Southern Highlands of Scotland.

Graeme Wallace

Waterfalls by Loch Lyon

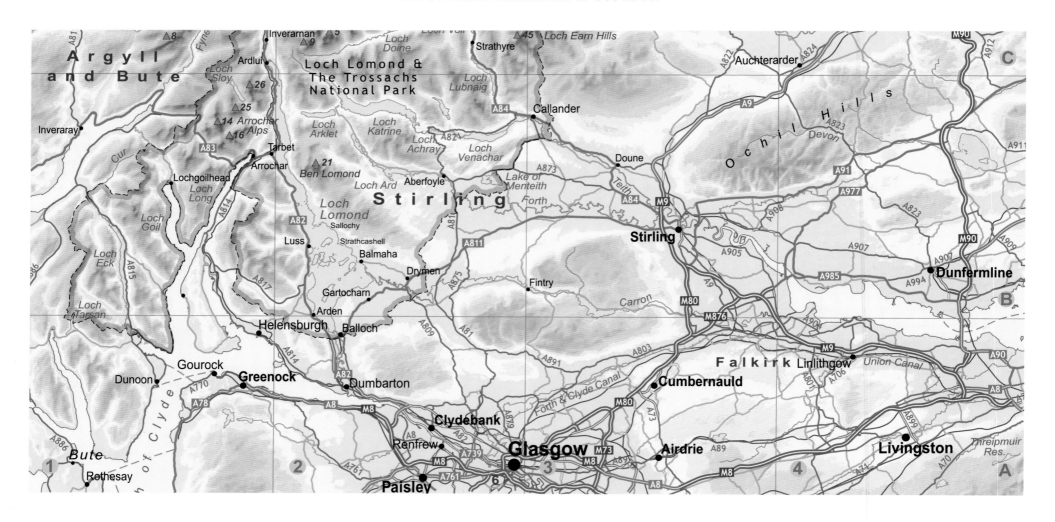

MUNROS

1 An Caisteal 995m - **C2**
2 An Stuc 1118m - **D3**
3 Beinn a' Chleibh 916m - **C1**
4 Beinn a' Chreachain 1081m - **D2**
5 Beinn a' Chroin 942m - **C2**
6 Beinn Achaladair 1038m - **C2**
7 Beinn an Dothaidh 1004m - **C1**
8 Beinn Bhuidhe 948m - **C1**
9 Beinn Chabhair 933m - **C2**
10 Beinn Dorain 1076m - **C1**

11 Beinn Dubhchraig 978m - **C1**
12 Beinn Ghlas 1103m - **C3**
13 Beinn Heasgarnich 1078m - **C2**
14 Beinn Ime 1011m - **B1**
15 Beinn Mhanach 953m - **C2**
16 Beinn Narnain 926m - **B1**
17 Beinn Tulaichean 946m - **C2**
18 Ben Challum 1025m - **C2**
19 Ben Chonzie 931m - **C3**
20 Ben Lawers 1214m - **C3**
21 Ben Lomond 974m - **B2**
22 Ben Lui 1130m - **C1**

23 Ben More 1174m - **C2**
24 Ben Oss 1029m - **C1**
25 Ben Vane 916m - **B1**
26 Ben Vorlich (Arrochar) 943m - **B1**
27 Ben Vorlich (Loch Earn) 985m - **C3**
28 Carn Gorm 1029m - **D2**
29 Carn Mairg 1041m - **D3**
30 Creag Mhor 1047m - **C2**
31 Cruach Ardrain 1046m - **C2**
32 Meall a' Choire Leith 926m - **D2**
33 Meall Buidhe 932m - **D2**
34 Meall Corranaich 1069m - **C2**

35 Meall Garbh (Glen Lyon) 968m - **D3**
36 Meall Garbh (Ben Lawers) 1118m - **D3**
37 Meall Ghaordaidh 1039m - **C2**
38 Meall Glas 959m - **C2**
39 Meall Greigh 1001m - **D3**
40 Meall nan Aighean 981m - **D3**
41 Meall nan Tarmachan 1043m - **C2**
42 Schiehallion 1083m - **D3**
43 Sgiath Chuil 921m - **C2**
44 Stob Binnein 1165m - **C2**
45 Stuc a' Chroin 975m - **C2**
46 Stuchd an Lochain 960m - **D2**

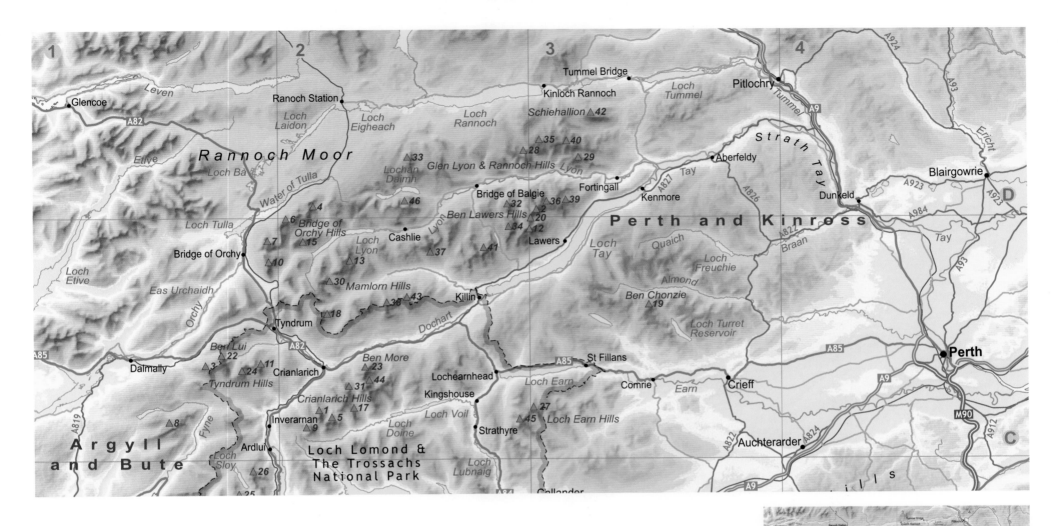

LOCHS

Loch Achray - **B2**
Loch Ard - **B2**
Loch Arklet - **B2**
Loch Ba - **D1**
Loch Doine - **C2**
Loch Earn - **C2/C3**
Loch Eigheach - **D2**
Loch Katrine - **B2**
Loch Laidon - **D2**
Loch Lomond - **B2**

Loch Long - **B1**
Loch Lubnaig - **B2/C2**
Loch Lyon - **C2**
Loch Rannoch - **D2/D3**
Loch Tay - **C2/C3/D3**
Loch Tulla - **C1**
Loch Tummel - **D4**
Loch Venachar - **B2**
Loch Voil - **C2**
Lochan Daimh - **D2**

BEINN LAOIGH (BEN LUI) 1130m - from BEN OSS, TYNDRUM

MEALL NAN TARMACHAN 1043m, and beyond to MEALL GHAORDAIDH 1039m - from BEINN GHLAS, BEN LAWERS HILLS

—— LOCH LOMOND AND INCHLONAIG ISLAND TO BEINN DUBH, ARROCHAR ALPS AND SUMMIT OF BEN LOMOND ON THE RIGHT - from CONIC HILL, BALMAHA——

THE TYNDRUM HILLS INCLUDING BEINN A' CHLEIBH 916m, BEN LUI 1130m, BEN OSS 1029m AND BEINN DUBHCHRAIG 978m - from TROISGEACH

BRIDGE OF ORCHY HILLS WITH BEINN DORAIN 1076m (FAR LEFT), AND MAMLORN HILLS WITH CREAG MHOR 1047m (CENTRE) AND BEN CHALLUM 1025m (RIGHT) - from BEINN DUBHCHRAIG

— LOOKING NORTH ALONG THE ALLT A' CHOBHAIR BURN TO CARN GORM 1029m, GLEN LYON HILLS WITH AN STUC 1118m AND THE BEN LAWERS RIDGE TO THE RIGHT —

THE CRIANLARICH HILLS ABOVE GLEN FALLOCH

STRATHCASHELL POINT, EAST OF LOCH LOMOND TO BEN LOMOND

MEALL CORRANAICH 1069m - from BEINN GHLAS, BEN LAWERS HILLS

North Loch Lomond to Ben Lomond 974m - from Troisgeach

—— Bridge of Orchy Hills with Beinn an Dothaidh 1004m, Beinn Achaladair 1038m, Beinn a' Chreachain 1081m and Beinn Mhanach 953m —— 35

BEN OSS 1029m AND BEN LUI 1130m - from BEINN A' CHAISTEIL

CLOUD INVERSION SHROUDING MEALL NAN TARMACHAN 1043m - from MEALL CORRANAICH, BEN LAWERS HILLS

Beinn Dorain 1076m - from Beinn a' Chaisteil, Bridge of Orchy

CRAINLARICH HILLS WITH BEN MORE, STOB BINNEIN, CRUACH ARDRAIN, BEINN TULAICHEAN, BEINN A' CHROIN, AN CAISTEAL AND BEINN CHABHAIR - from BEINN DUBHCHRAIG

BEN LAWERS 1214m AND THE BEN LAWERS RIDGE ACROSS from MEALL CORRANAICH

Loch Lyon with Beinn Mhanach 953m (left) and Beinn a' Chreachain 1081m (distant left)

The Loch Lomond islands of Inchfad, Inchcruin, Bucinch, Inchconnachan and Inchlonaig to the hills of Glen Luss

CLOUD COVERED BRIDGE OF ORCHY HILLS INCLUDING BEINN A' CHREACHAIN, BEINN ACHALADAIR AND BEINN AN DOTHAIDH - from LOCH BA

LOCH LOMOND SUNSET - from CONIC HILL, BALMAHA

Mist filled glens of Tyndrum and Crianlarich with snow capped Ben Lui - from Stob a' Choire Odhair, near Bridge of Orchy

BEN LOMOND 974m - from BEINN DUBH, ABOVE LUSS

MEALL MOR REFLECTED IN LOCH LUBNAIG, NEAR KILMAHOG

THE ARROCHAR ALPS BEYOND LOCH ARKLET, THE TROSSACHS

Mist shrouded Loch Dochart Castle, near Crianlarich

SUMMIT OF BEN LOMOND 974m

BEINN NARNAIN 926m AND BEN ARTHUR TO SOUTHERN LOCH LOMOND HILLS - from BEINN IME, ARROCHAR ALPS

SUNRISE OVER LOCH KATRINE - from STRONACHLACHAR

ARROCHAR ALPS ABOVE LOCH LOMOND AND LOCH LONG WITH THE HIGHLIGHTED SNOW CAPPED PEAK OF BEINN IME 1011m - from BEN LOMOND

SUNSET BEHIND LOCH EARN - from ST FILLANS

The Glen Lyon Hills with Carn Mairg 1041m - from Schiehallion

THE PINNACLE, BEN ARTHUR (THE COBBLER), ARROCHAR ALPS, WITH BEN LOMOND (DISTANT LEFT)

SUNSET BEYOND THE HILLS ALONG GLEN ORCHY

EARLY MORNING MIST HANGING OVER LOCH DOINE, LEADING ONTO LOCH VOIL

BEN MORE 1174m AND STOB BINNEIN 1165m - from BEINN TULAICHEAN, CRIANLARICH HILLS

KAYAK ON LOCH VENACHAR, THE TROSSACHS

Snow residual on Beinn Heasgarnich 1078m - from Glen Lyon

SUNSET OVER LOCH RANNOCH - from SCHIEHALLION

ACROSS LOCH LOMOND TO HILLS BEHIND LUSS - from BALMAHA

SEA OF MIST OVER LOCH TAY, ACROSS TO BEN VORLICH & STUC A' CHROIN - from BEINN GHLAS

STUC A' CHROIN 975m - from BEN VORLICH

SUNRISE OVER LOCH EARN - from BEN VORLICH

YACHTS AT ANCHOR AT BALMAHA

FALLS OF DOCHART, KILLIN

Ben Lomond 974m above low lying cloud over Loch Lomond

LOCH LONG AND THE VILLAGE OF ARROCHAR - from CRUACH TAIRBEIRT

LOCH LOMOND from ARDLUI

MEALL GHAORDAIDH 1039m (IN SHADOW) AND STUCHD AN LOCHAIN 960m (CENTRE) ABOVE LOCH AN DAIMH - from MEALL A' CHOIRE LEITH

THATCHED COTTAGES AT FORTINGALL

GLEN FALLOCH TO MEALL DHAMH AND CRUACH ARDRAIN 1046m, CRIANLARICH

CLOUD SHROUDED BEN LAWERS 1214m AND AN STUC 1118m - from MEALL GARBH

SCHIEHALLION 1083m - from LOCH KINARDOCHY

MEALL BUIDHE 932m ABOVE LOCH AN DAIMH - from STUCHD AN LOCHAIN

An Stuc 1118m above Lochan nan Cat, Ben Lawers Hills

SRON GHARBH (CENTRE) LEADING TO AN CAISTEAL 995m (BEHIND) - from GLEN FALLOCH

LOCH TUMMEL AND SCHIEHALLION - from QUEEN'S VIEW

BEINN HEASGARNICH 1078m (CENTRE LEFT) AND BEYOND TO BEN CHALLUM AND THE MAMLORN HILLS - from STUCHD AN LOCHAIN, GLEN LYON

LOCH KATRINE ALONG GLEN GYLE, THE TROSSACHS

WATERFALLS AT EAS URCHAIDH, RIVER ORCHY

BEN VENUE REFLECTED IN LOCH ACHRAY, THE TROSSACHS

FALLS OF FALLOCH, GLEN FALLOCH

LOCH LOMOND SUNSET - from GARTOCHARN

Heavy mist hanging over Loch Lomond

BEINN HEASGARNICH 1078m, MAMLORN HILLS – From GLEN LYON

LOCH KATRINE LEADING TO SNOW CAPPED CRIANLARICH HILLS - from BEN A'AN

BEINN BHUIDHE (948m) ABOVE GLEN FYNE - from PORTSONACHAN

LOCH VENACHAR SUNSET, THE TROSSACHS

LOCH TULLA WITH BEINN ACHALADAIR 1038m AND BEINN AN DOTHAIDH 1004m, BRIDGE OF ORCHY

BEN A'AN ABOVE LOCH KATRINE WITH CRIANLARICH HILLS ON THE HORIZON

DAWN AT SALLOCHY, EAST LOCH LOMOND

GLEN LYON WITH THE GLEN LYON HILLS TO THE LEFT AND THE BEN LAWERS HILL TO THE RIGHT

THE GLEN LYON HILLS (CENTRE) AND SCHIEHALLION (RIGHT) - from GLEN QUAICH

OAK TREE AT BALQUHIDDER

BEN ARTHUR (THE COBBLER) WITH BEINN NARNAIN 926m AND BEINN IME 1011m, ARROCHAR ALPS

BEN MORE 1174m - from CRIANLARICH

TARMACHAN RIDGE - from FALLS OF DOCHART, KILLIN

BEN LOMOND 974m - from TULLICH HILL

BEINN TULAICHEAN 946m - from LOCH VOIL

BEN CHALLUM 1025m - from CRIANLARICH

Beinn Ghlas 1103m, Ben Lawers 1214m, An Stuc 1118m, Meall Garbh 1118m and Meall Greigh 1001m - from Loch Tay

BEN MORE 1174m ABOVE CRIANLARICH RAILWAY STATION

LOCH LOMOND SUNSET OVER INCHCAILLOCH AND TORRINCH ALONG THE HIGHLAND BOUNDARY FAULT - from CONIC HILL

INDEX